2004

THE MORNING OF THE
RED ADMIRALS

OTHER BOOKS BY ROBERT DANA

POETRY

Summer   *2000*

Hello, Stranger   *1996*

Yes, Everything   *1994*

What I Think I Know: New & Selected Poems   *1991*

Starting Out For The Difficult World   *1987*

In A Fugitive Season   *1980*

The Power Of The Visible   *1971*

Some Versions Of Silence   *1967*

PROSE

A Community of Writers: Paul Engle & The Iowa
Writers' Workshop   *1999*

Against The Grain: Interviews With Maverick
American Publishers   *1986*

LIMITED EDITIONS

Wildebeest   *1993*

Blood Harvest   *1986*

What The Stones Know   *1982*

In A Fugitive Season   *1979*

Journeys From The Skin   *1966 (pamphlet)*

The Dark Flags Of Waking   *1964*

My Glass Brother And Other Poems   *1957 (pamphlet)*

THE MORNING OF THE
RED ADMIRALS

ROBERT
DANA

ANHINGA PRESS, 2004
TALLAHASSEE, FLORIDA

Copyright © Robert Dana 2004

All rights reserved under
International and Pan-American Copyright Conventions.

No portion of this book may be reproduced in any form without
the written permission of the publisher, except by a reviewer,
who may quote brief passages in connection with a review
for a magazine or newspaper.

This publication is sponsored in part by a grant from the Florida Department of
State, Division of Cultural Affairs, and the Florida Arts Council.

Cover art: Photographs of the Red Admiral butterfly
        Robert B. Srygley and Adrian Thomas, University of Oxford, UK
Author photo: Peg Dana
Cover design, book design, and production: C.L. Knight

Library of Congress Cataloging-in-Publication Data
The Morning of the Red Admirals by Robert Dana – First Edition
ISBN 0938078-78-X (cloth)
ISBN 0938078-77-1 (paper)
Library of Congress Cataloging Card Number – 2004100004

Anhinga Press Inc. is a nonprofit corporation dedicated wholly
to the publication and appreciation of fine poetry.

For personal orders, catalogs and information write to:
Anhinga Press
P.O. Box 10595
Tallahassee, FL 32302
Web site: www.anhinga.org
E-mail: info@anhinga.org

Published in the United States by Anhinga Press, Tallahassee, Florida.
First Edition, 2004

For Sister Mary, my sister,
who prays for us all

ACKNOWLEDGMENTS

My thanks to the editors of the following magazines in which these poems first appeared:

Another Chicago Magazine: "Of Cats, Switchblades & The Unimaginable," "Spindrift," "Stepping Lightly," and "Ten Thousand Wingbeats Five Hundred Heartbeats"

The Chariton Review: "The Knot" and "Killing The Yellowjackets"

The Chattahoochee Review: "Walking The Yellow Dog" and "Waking In Connecticut"

Controlled Burn: "Garden Fable"

The Georgia Review: "Mercy, Perhaps" and "The Morning of the Red Admirals"

Hampden-Sydney Review: "Clear" and "Exit"

High Plains Literary Review: "Merciless Grace"

The Iowa Review: "This Time"

The Marlboro Review: "February"

Monthly Review: "In Heaven"

New Letters: ".com"

The North American Review: "Fireworks"

The Prairie Schooner: "The Figures" and "Light"

Smartish Pace: "Tropic Freeze"

Tampa Review: "Bird of Paradise," "Chimes," "Kaliban on Estero," and "Late October Rainy Days"

CONTENTS

… it is all or nothing in this life, for there is no other.
— Larry Levis

THE MORNING OF THE RED ADMIRALS

for D & L

We saw them first
        last evening — two,
spiralling up
        a column of late
sunlight, then,
        tilting away
from each other
        in a floating stagger
through the early
        summer leaves —
a jittery dipping,
        dropping, rising —
one coming
        to rest a moment
on the still warm
        roof of our fat
pagoda lantern,
        the other on weathered
deck rail;
        the tips of its
long antennae
        beaded and bright;
wings black,
        white dot
and blue dot,
        and barred aslant
with orange red,
        laid flat,
then clicking shut
        to dull grey sail,
then opening again.

Now, it's morning;
        you've gone to work.
The air gleams,
        dry and clear,
almost Greek,
        and a half dozen
admirals sip
        from the lilac blossoms,
still signalling
        their unsayable
story. One
        lights on my shoulder
as I hang the day's
        laundry on the line,
shirts and drawers,
        dull socks,
our flapping colors
        answering his.
He's weightless,
        this migrant —
a small, wild
        scrap of grace —
and I'm his resting
        post on the way
to whatever far
        edge of creation
breathes at the tips
        of his wings.

I. WALKING THE YELLOW DOG

WALKING THE YELLOW DOG

You see them walking,
the woman and the dog,
a long, curving concourse
in a park, perhaps
by a river; city buildings,
perhaps, in the distance
to the left and right.
You can't be sure
of much of anything,
the two by two and a half
inch reproduction,
in the Friday *Times,*
of a larger photograph,
being muddy and badly
out of register.
The dog appears to be
the yellow white old
golden retriever mixes
get; and the woman,
seen from the back,
seems middle-aged
in her jeans, jean
jacket, and short pony
tail, her hair grey
or dishwater blonde.
The leaves or blossoms
on branches overhead
are dark and blotty,
and the faint hint of pink
on the horizon behind
the dissolving buildings —
either a printer's error,
or sunrise, or evening.

Back in the kitchen
of her little clapboard
house or studio apartment,
a crude, hand carved
and painted, life sized
Sacred Heart flames
beside the phone,
the ends of its rainbow
of satin streamers tipped
with *milagros, milagritos,*
the little miracles
we sometimes pray for.
The flag of the dog's
tail seems happy,
and his bark has mastered
all the bad reproduction,
reduction, and cropping —
now writ large, either
as this miniature of The Great
American Loneliness,
or of love and compassion
and duty finely balanced;
or the perfect composure
of our photographer's eye.

.COM

My neighbor across the street
and down, died this morning.
Of colon cancer. Ending
four months of watching
birds in his back yard,
and eating ice cream, his pain
dumbed by a morphine drip
so carefully calibrated
only a machinist, which
he was, could fully
appreciate it. And his wife.
Such a fine and terrible
day to close out a life.
The first morning, really,
you could see your breath;
sunlight slicking every
still-green leaf. The air
windless, brisk, and edgy.

Then, the white van. Not
a hearse. A plain white
van in the drive. No
lettering at all. Just
two men. One in an uncle's
tired brown suit; his bulky
companion in shirtsleeves
following; both walking
as if in bedroom slippers;
wheeling their gurney up
the lawn to the rear of the house
through the sparkling dew,
past the red geraniums
and drifts of pink *impatiens* —
www.death.com

It's early. No children
maunder yet toward their
orange bus. And young
couples, behind the closed
doors of their duplexes,
ready themselves for a day's
work. Not a car passes.
In such suburbs, no
aproned women approach
death's door bearing
covered dishes. Later,
I'll remember how he gave
away his last precision
tools. And still later,
bedroom shades will be
raised, windows opened,
and air enter the house,
and light, and silence.

CLEAR

A roll of fog
snug along the river
and the little ponds
steaming, and the big
sun rising in its
unspeakable glory;
a hawk launches
silently from a nearby
tree, glides without
haste across a great
stand of goldenrod,
then banks slightly
down the valley
out of sight. The sky's
a deep, hard
blue, and cloudless.

WAKING IN CONNECTICUT

I heard a bird calling in the darkness of morning in Connecticut.
    It wasn't a cry I knew.
And I lay awake then the long hours until first light,
    but he didn't call again.
All I heard was a woodpecker rapping out in a hard code
    his own ecstatic measure.
And beside me, still in a warm cloud of sleep, my wife,
    her breathing regular and easy.

THE FIGURES

In memoriam:
Stephen Lacey, 1943-2000

Sunday morning. A summery
March 26th, and I'm pastor
again of The Little Church
Of Last Year's Fallen Leaves.
Mostly oak. Mostly white.
Some red. Some burr. Those
plastered together closest
to the dirt make up a black,
wet page. Text for a late
mass, perhaps. My raking,
a late call to prayer.
My parishioners, the usual
ones for the time of year:
the beetle, the hellgrammite,
the robin, the mole. My own
work's a kind of sweat
meditation. Join me. It's
the perfect weather for it,
and the clearing out will
go faster. By noon, we'll
lie back on a hill of grass,
the beer tasting crisper,
the crackers saltier than
we might ever have imagined.
And though I cannot now
know it, tomorrow, a young
friend will die of pulmonary
honeycomb fibrosis, as if
some strain of bees, finding
him choice enough to hive in,
drowned him in their sweetness.

Later, oh much, much later,
should you choose to read
in your *Book of Hours,*
look no further. You know
those figures in the old story,
aflame at the edge of the wood.

LIGHT

At six, the kitchen glows with June
morning light. It doesn't pour down
between the slanting beams, or burst
through the high clerestoreys. It's
simply there — luminous volume —
as if a god had entered the room
and still lingered, unmoving,
purposeless. I'm sure, as a lonely
Irish Catholic boy, one of the padre's
favorites for early morning altar
duty, standing in a chill sacristy,
I might have thought so. An old
man, now, I know there is no god,
that this light's his only voice.

PERFECT

Three and three and three.
Hats in the hat store window.
Ducks on the water.

KOAN

To make from slightness
a beam of such sweet steel

bendable as light

There's a light that shines from the young

from within, that's like no other.

As if timelessness took up physical form.

As if, had the morning a word for itself

and could stay, it would speak this one.

GARDEN FABLE

Aristoxenus, the Hedonist,
watered his lettuce with wine
and honey, knowing the difference
between nothing and something
is not just something, but some-
thing special. And wondering
whether such knowledge
was wisdom or commonplace,
conundrum or cloud, I watch,
through long afternoons,
the cloud-furnaces building,
the storms rumbling in
on great drays, scrapes
of lightning, temperatures
dropping; then, the air white
with water falling, sluicing
gutters; the pelts of trees
sodden. And later, the sun
lighting it. The work that
humbles the body. The sheer
sheen and weight of longing,
the delicious ache of it.

ECSTASY

I'm on a White Lady high
behind the wheel of my car.
No, I'm not a racist,
and this has nothing to do
with women. Let's keep
talking beyond the facts.
Let's keep waking
from sleep into ecstasy.
I mean the real thing.
It's not a pill, it's a peach,
tell them. Just as addictive,
but with no bad side-effects
other than sweet, wet
pleasure that overflows
your mouth and runs down
your chin and between your
breasts or soaks your shirt
pocket, and leaves your
hands sticky with the nectar
we *should* get busted for.

EXIT

85 down Highway 6,
the Grand Army Highway,
headed west. I glimpse
two small ducks
hurrying up along
the surface of a pond;
blue- or green-winged
teal, surely, so-called
for the broad half
chevron at their shoulders,
blue or green, bordered
above and below with white,
like regimental stripes.
Now, I'm ducking in
and out from behind combines,
tractor-drawn wagons;
then, banking and heeling
the sloping and rising
curves beyond Newton;
a cloud of water rising
to my right: a road
expiring in its plume
of dust. Later, down
Interstate 80, I race
on in the rage and howl
of 18-wheelers, vans,
rusted pickups, storming
on toward the exit
to those two storied
towns, Peace and Quiet.

A summer of failures, one
after another, it would seem.
I thought I'd killed a nest
of yellowjackets, filling
their hole in the ground
with poison just at dark,
then tamping it with dirt
to close it. For the next
three days, I felt bad
about it. Each dusk, I'd
look at that dull stamp
of earth and feel regret;
miss their honey-colored
whirr as they came and went,
ascending and descending
vertically, then streaking
out and back and out.
Once, as a boy, back in
New England, from atop
a boulder wall beside
a fishing brook, I raced
away across razor
hay-stubble, stung a hot
half dozen times, leaving
my new sneakers soaking
wet there until nightfall.
As it turns out, I've no
reason to get sentimental.
They're back today, their
nest-hole bigger than
before. What now? Kill
them with a new, more
powerful poison? One

that will remain in dirt
and grass for years? Or
let them be until frost.
Right now, nothing works.
My usually profligate
garden, drifted in late
spring with herbicide
by some local lawn-care
outfit, shows only a few
tiny, green tomatoes.
I've pulled up the beans.
Empty pods. Their vines
pallid as sick string.
Leaves riddled to lace
by unkillable beetles.
And no poems. Just
this one that doesn't quite
work, and a stack of shapeless
prose. All of it headed,
surely, to the burning barrel
and the compost heap.

Not snow. Moonlight
fills the woods. The
grand spill of leaves;
trees falling, standing;
the felled, dismembered,
hundred-year-old oak;
scrub rinsed in a thin
cemeterial light;
souls passing in both
directions, or passing away,
in this not quite night
not yet quite day.

FEBRUARY

1.
Winter drags on
toward spring.
Freeze and thaw,
sleet and freeze.
Ground still hard.
Armor of ice,
grey and runnelled
under the trees.

2.
On Christmas day,
a fledgling Redtail
killed a rabbit
just below this
window, splashing
the bright snow
with blood. Now,
like weak smoke
from a cold fire,
dishevelled fur
slubs up through
the bitten drift.

3.
Down the deadfall
stream, a sudden
synod of crows
in glossy, severest
black bickers
and preaches, flapping
from bare branch
to branch, their
contradictions crying,
echoing, fading.

4.
And tonight, off
Holiday Road,
in the sub-zero
moonlight of his
memorial, who
will cheer him
down his frozen
ladder? — bronze-
jacketed, -booted,
-helmeted volunteer
fireman, a child
in the crook of his
arm — down,
under the icy
fire of the stars.

THE KNOT

March 21st. One day
after the vernal equinox.
Second day of spring.
Jackstraws of frost
tumble up the glass
of my rented window.
It's six above. Sunny.
But the sun packs
no kick, no heat. And
the little rail lines
of crystals tracking west
across the pane, pinched
and fuzzy, catawampus,
weave the skewed web
of a drugged spider.

My room looks out on
the back of The Church
of Doubting Thomas
where the faithful enter
at odd hours by the back
door, and an iron
starling never flies
from its black perch
above fifty yards
of frozen water hose.

In a small winter-
shattered garden off
to the side, a larger
than life-size Blessed
Virgin prays relent-
lessly, day and night,
a broadsword rising

from between her feet,
upward along her thighs
to a point just below
her breasts; its hilt
strung with a stone
rosary, beads joined
at the crucifix; her
sparrows warming them-
selves in her arbor
and on the shallow stone
abutments of the church.

A man in the blue shirt
and suspendered, dark blue
trousers of Maintenance
opens the door now
and sweeps some dust
and grit onto the bitten,
already dirty snow.
He pays no attention
to the wind whipping
sea-green salt crystals
from the walkway, the
tumbled bird basin,
the cocked lattice where
a dormant vine signs
its wicked Celtic knot.

MERCY, PERHAPS

Tonight, an old friend called
from L.A. to say her ex-
husband's set to marry one
of the Doublemint Girls
whose 17-year-old daughter
he sent up for prostitution.
A Twenty-first Century,
West Coast romance.

*

Elsewhere, the world
and its children grow
more murderous;
the blood-soaked beast
dervishing in spiritual drag
in every broken,
dusty, public square;
damning its offspring
unto the last generation.

*

Nobody's innocent.
Temporarily displaced
by movers, my wife and I
have bedded down
in my study amid shelf-loads
of wonders, lies, and hatreds —
on the old pull-out couch,
its mattress thin as misery.

We're sleeping, now, between
the cricket and the mouse.
Or trying to. The cricket's
just tuned up his tiny bells
for a celebration he's about
to play. Beside my right ear,
in the bookcase, the mouse
is dining on the pages
of someone's biography, one
whose author's name
occurs late in the alphabet
— does it? — with T or Y.

It's 4 a.m. When we wake
in a couple of hours,
we'll arise, shower
in sweet, clear water,
dress, and drink coffee
gritty and black. Then,
we'll kiss farewell
and set out once again
in the green and sunlit
or grey day, each
in our own direction,
to do a decent piece
of work. We'll inflict
no pain, maybe find
small justice, compassion.
Mercy, perhaps.

THIS TIME

A click. A bright wink. Lightning
out of a plain, grey midmorning sky,
as if the day had snapped its fingers.

Then how many long seconds of silence?
You realize you're not breathing.
"Jesus," you think, "they've got a nuke."

And in your mind's eye you see it,
swaying under its parachute as it floats
down. Then, the click, the twinkle.

You lower the half-read newspaper
to your lap, consider yellow autumn.
And then a roar like no other,

as if the earth itself had split open,
shuddering from its foundations.
You wait for the shock wave, the storm

of window glass, the firewind, that
microsecond before darkness blooms
simultaneously and everywhere.

But only blessed, ordinary rain
begins to fall. By lunch time, light
redeems the woods, the quiet street.

Your cat, Miss Futzy, emerges from
her shelter under your old desk.
Washed and preened now, she sits

upright and solid as a doorstop
or one of those classic Egyptian tomb
cats you see in the museums.

A black sun in the white sky of her
back, and an evening cloud coming on.
A black moon riding her right shoulder.

The calm regard of her green eyes.

II. IN PANAMA

I've never been in Panama.

But I have a taste for the tropics. I served in the Navy as a radio operator on Guam at the end of World War II. The jungle ran down to the beaches back then, and the beaches were empty and beautiful, the water crystalline. And the locals who dynamited fish in the early mornings were gone by the time we baled out of our jeep for a baptismal dip.

I lived in Mexico for half a year back in the 1960's with my first wife, my two daughters, ages five and seven, and my six-week-old son. But despite the fact that our courtyard boasted a lime tree and bougain-villea in profusion, we were not in the tropics. The climate in Chapala, south of Guadalajara, was mountain dry, and often cool, like Denver.

Visiting friends in Barbados not so long ago, I felt pretty much at home.

I've written next to nothing about the South Pacific and nothing at all about Mexico or Barbados. And the tropics that fringed the great sea that once covered the Midwest where I live all disappeared millions of years ago.

Panama has to do with change.

*

In August of 1998, I finished a poem entitled "The Morning of the Red Admirals." The poem was triggered by a pair of these butterflies spiraling together up a column of late evening sunlight in our woods.

My wife and I got up from our gin and tonics and stood by the deck rail to get a better look at them. The variety of their movements was uncommon in our experience, and we watched them closely until they sailed away and the light faded.

There was a time when I was a serious amateur lepidopterist. I was probably twelve or thirteen then and lived in a part of our town known as The Patch. I came under the tutelage of Johnny Pavelchek, an older boy who lived just up the street with his aunt. Johnny was a natural naturalist. Behind his back, with a mixture of admiration, envy, and contempt, people called him The Sportsman. He was already an excellent trout fisherman, known for getting his limit when no one else was getting even a rise. He'd saved what little money he came by and bought a beautiful split bamboo rod. He also tied most of his own flies, and taught me how to. Perhaps my first brush with a painstaking art. He also fired my passion for butterflies, showing me how to catch them without damaging them, how to kill and mount them. And, most important, of course, how to identify them. Johnny may have been my first brush with seriousness.

I lived many of those hot and muggy New England days, roaming the summer hills, woods, and hayfields in hopes of spotting a mourning cloak or a blue hairstreak or a zebra swallowtail.

So the visit of the red admirals inadvertently stirred an old, old passion.

*

At about that time, I'd also grown restless with the poetry I'd been writing.

This fit comes over me at times in my life when I feel I've mastered a certain range of subject matter and a certain way of writing about it. In any era, poets, some even famous masters, often turn out basically the same kind of poem year after year. Indeed, editors and readers know, generally, what to expect from writers whose work they return to again and again, and the fulfillment of that expectation is part of their pleasure. Thus, what's meant, when we talk of a writer's style is this immediately identifiable way of marshalling language around a favored and familiar subject.

We can all recognize a page of Frost, or Auden, or Elizabeth Bishop, or Robert Lowell probably. We can all recognize one of Berryman's *Dream Songs*, but not quite so easily, perhaps, one of his sonnets or late prayers.

Unlike many of the great masters whose work I love, after a time I want to push on past my "style," to some new way of seeing and hearing and talking. To invoke a new rhythm, a new timing. For a very long time, I've wanted a poetry that was less compositional and more improvisational. Less predictable. To this end, I have made and unmade several styles for different books, exploring possibilities. Perhaps like the Portuguese poet Fernando Pessoa, I should have published the books under different names. Like Pessoa, probably I will die in obscurity because I have no recognizable signature or trademark. Anyone can see, for example, that the poems in this book might have been written by two different poets.

(It occurs to me that what I just wrote about my having no signature style may not be entirely true. It may be that it's less than obvious from book to book, more shifting, that it goes in many guises.)

*

In any case, the red admirals disappeared with the season, the years passed, poems large and small slowly piled up, some in one style, others in another. Then, in 2002, four years after the first visit of the red admirals, an article appeared in *The New York Times* for December 12. Two British scientists working at the Smithsonian Tropical

Research Institute in Panama had made some remarkable discoveries about how butterflies fly. The star of the show turned out to be *Vanessa atalanta,* the red admiral.

First of all, the red admiral used all four of the known wing strokes used by flying insects. The names of some of the strokes and their aftermaths offer a kind of poetry themselves: clap and fling, wake capture, stopping vortex. But more surprising was the discovery that the admiral, unlike any other butterfly, improvised the order of its strokes freshly every time, never repeating itself. "If the average human being moved like the average red admiral," James Gorman wrote in the *Times,* "city sidewalks would be filled with people progressing by hop, skip, jump, cartwheel, and back flip, in no particular order."

My kind of butterfly. My kind of poem on the wing.

Indeed, the whole experience involving *Vanessa atalanta* has been accidental, coincidental, unplanned — improvisational in the best sense.

*

These last few days, I've been trying to close the book, so to speak, on the red admiral. But the simplest questions are the most difficult to answer it would seem. Perhaps that's a general rule, a universal truth.

Where did the admiral class of butterflies get its name? Search where you will, you will not find an answer. Apparently, the common, everyday names for plants and insects are made up by persons with an intense dislike or affection for them. They may or may not have any root in the truth or bear any resemblance to reality. The red admiral, for instance, is a butterfly dominated by slanting orange bars and broken white bars on black wings tipped with blue. Even if we call the color red-orange, it could hardly be mistaken for red.

Since *admiral* is an English word, it may be presumed that someone English, a very long time ago, saw some quality about the insect that suggested something nautical—perhaps in the colors, or the way the colors were arrayed. Certainly not in the shape of its sails. Perhaps the word was originally *admirable* and later became corrupted to *admiral*, language changing mistakenly in the mouth of the speaker or the ear of the hearer as it often does. Almost certainly, no one employed the etymology of either word. Both derive from the Arabic *amir al* meaning ruler or commander, as in *amir-al-bahr*: commander of the sea. And the red admiral could fairly be said to command the air. Butterfly itself is a word about which *The Oxford English Dictionary* says only "The reason of the name is unknown."

Linnaeus classified and cataloged the species in 1758, as nearly as I can make out. At one time, he was offered the post of naval surgeon in his native Sweden and turned it down. In any case, he can hardly be the originator of the English name, although he's probably responsible for the butterfly's formal scientific designation as *Vanessa atalanta*.

The designation is properly and scientifically Greek: Vanessa [*Phanaessa*] being the ancient Greek word for butterfly, and Atalanta recalling the myth in which a woman of that name, famed for being swift of foot, is tricked into marrying her suitor when he drops golden apples that distract her from her determination to beat him and thus remain single.

It's pure speculation, of course, but did Linnaeus see some parallel between the admiral's staggering flight and Atalanta's erratic run? It's unlikely we'll ever know. It's not the sort of information entomologists probably regard as central.

*

So here I am with my butterflies and my book.

I don't think the book contains any perfect poems, but that's all right. "The achievement of perfection is the road to silence," Robert Lowell wrote, and I'm not ready for silence yet.

In any case, look for me, Reader, in the dapple of these lines, in the late-summer morning or evening of these poems. And look for the butterfly, dipping and slanting and jagging little flashes of color into the air on its jazzy stagger toward whatever far edge of creation may still be breathing out there.

III. TEN THOUSAND WINGBEATS
FIVE HUNDRED HEARTBEATS

FIVE CARD DRAW

Ace bloweth where he listeth.

King blow west.

Queen blow in from the east
bumping up clouds and lightning. Rain.

Wolf show up with a man's whole hand in his mouth.

Yellow eyes.

Red Jack wink, say nuthin', an' move on.

BIRD OF PARADISE

Vast cracked flood of salt and tears.

Is it true we must be brave or risk pity?

*

But the sea's a very odd story.

This morning at sunrise, it furls itself brightly along the shore.

Long strings of glassy beads, bubbly abacus
on which we tote up our thoughts.

*

Yes, I'm your old opposer.
My shoulder always pushing against the absolute proposition.

My head full of winks of sunlight.

*

Can you see the Sunday bikers in their black leathers,
faces masked by black balaclavas against the chill,
helmets and buckles and studs gleaming;

rolling down San Carlos on their Goldwings and Harleys?

Can you hear the explosions of their engines when they throttle up?
Barbarous Beethoven, its industrial measures perfectly timed.

*

Purposeless beauty.

*

The sea, a sheet of diamonds.

*

Each thing being what it is by proving itself necessarily that.

*

The red tide about which we know less than we know about the blood.
The dead small hammerheads on the beach, their tails raked for speed,
the winged ray, the eyeless mullet.

The German girl, Mika, once sold into slavery in Syria.

*

Nothing not literal.

What we want is that folding out from the center,
that muscular push.

The flower. The fire.

To embody.

*

Why
dear friend, lover, I can think of you only in the particular.

*

It's night now.
The sea's breathing labors in the dark, air conditioners hum,
the lights of Naples twinkle far down the curving coast.

A stranger's voice calls across the empty terrace.

KALIBAN ON ESTERO

Slack-souled walker.

                    Mind of wind. Morning's
Slate-green waters. Constant shape-shifter.

*

Yes, I believe that.

*

Beauty is sometimes slender, fine faced.
An outrageousness made small and quiet.

*

Seeing clearly the long chilly miles north, the bridge,
low white span from mainland to island. Shore rentals.
Homes of the rich.

How Bluebill Realty will fluctuate profitably.

*

Two days ago, off Big Carlos,
a boy's body, blue and stiff,
borne away from his father's flipped skiff in fast current.

*

The eternally hungry herring-gulls screech us off the beach.

*

Where's dread?

Whisperer, this is not about you.

Evening spreads its sumptuous robes.

Ring the cold sea.
Toll the big honeybell of the sun.

The wind heebie-jeebies.

*

Where's the bread of silence that can be torn and eaten?

As children we mistook it for boredom and emptiness.

*

Now, it's disappeared in all directions flat as time.
A beaten tissue.

*

What's more perfect than two pelicans staggered and soaring?
Three pelicans.

Then, a fourth, trailing.

Sliding into the turning formation smoothly as a bead on a silk string.

*

Bark, Silence! Play the dog.

The brown Doberman retrieving his stick from the waves.

Dripping and frisking,
wheeling and cantering long-strided and loose-legged on the sand.

*

Cage thought all noise music.

Perhaps silence is the natural language of nothing.

*

So many, sooner or later, come to the shore.

*

I've walked with them morning and evening —
The young and the old —

Tasting their loneliness.

The waiting.

The place they've come to not entirely familiar.

*

Perhaps I no longer love poetry.
So much of it's banal now, and mannered and pretentious and stupid.

-biz.

Better to go in rags.

*

Under the palms,
two brown old women sit smoking and gossiping.

As they have every day every year since their husbands died.

As they will every year until *they* do.

*

I'm trying to find a place here
for that dirty run-down flat-roofed one-story concrete block house

behind the tattoo parlor.

Now cleaned up and painted two gorgeous shades of French lavender.
With a new yellow door.

And in front,
crouched in morning shade, a dark yellow sports car.

*

Well, don't just sit there. Help me.

TROPIC FREEZE

Low chop of the Gulf,
                    sun spangled,

strewn and a-jingle with living silver.

And south,
the two or three high-rise condo towns that weigh down the shore,
already fading in the heat-haze.

                              *

What if it's all
just hiss and a blue flash?

What if it's my friend's Dhawo dark mustachioed and argumentative
striding toward us across the air,
chewing the stub of the last good five-cent panatela?

What if the afternoon
coughs up a long white fishbone of cloud?

                              *

My left hand is schooled to pain.
My right to pleasure.

And age comes like a stumble.

I think of the blank world,
                              never far off
about which we know nothing.

A world, at best, probably, of clicks and snaps and rattles.
                                                  Winks.

At worst, a boredom of silence and darkness and stillness.

*

Not this.
Not here.
Where oranges deepen their sweetness tonight
                                        in the unseasonable freeze.

And by day,
pelicans read that slip of air just above the water with their wingtips
as they slide for miles along the shallows.

And the traveler tree unfolds its elegant fan.

*

Beauty in my version of the fable is The Beast and the beast is glory.

*

So dinch me on,
                    my darlings.
Dance me down

this senseless, bright dingle of commingling and delicious confusions.

FIREWORKS

This is the silver hour.

The sun crowning in the high cusps of the oaks.
Its light spilling down over the cascading leaves.

An elegance old and European.

The trees, all of them —
the oaks, mulberry, dogwoods & wild cherries,
the shagbarks & hackberrys —

from seeds brought here in the pockets of immigrants,
                                        the beaks of birds.

Over the years,
scattering windbreaks, small civilities of shade
                            across smothering prairie —

a thousand miles of grass
so tall you could tie it across your saddle horn.

                    *

Frozen stars.

My gin and tonic frets and fizzes in its glass lit by a slice of lemon.

From somewhere, murmurs.

The cries of faraway children.
Neighbors at their Thursday night Bible meeting.

Low highway surf.

Algorithms of what?

*

I've become a lesson.

A poem on the page of a calendar for use in schools.
A list of questions.

Well, that's new.

"Ask students to list places they would write their names."
"Ask 'What means a lot to you?'"
"Ask students 'What color is the spirit?'"

*

The randomness of simple systems computes to infinite complexity,
we're told.

There's no stopping.
And there are no shortcuts.

All systems must be played out through thousands of generations.

Alive on the breath-edge of metaphor.

Alive in the bird-chat of the sweetness of oncoming evening.
Waiting for the wonder of darkness.

*

And in the mornings,
or through the long, heavy, rumpled heat of early summer afternoons,

my shadow cat,
invisible,
        reclining amid the iridescence, the pelluscence of certain roses.

How many generations of randomness to the pattern that ignites

that inner light,
that transparency?

The whole garden exploding like a sky of Chinese fireworks.

*

The elegant lady's gone.
Her intelligence and her decencies.

I saw her dressed impeccably yesterday like a doll of age.
Saw the cover closed gently on her as the cover of a favorite book is closed.

Then, the expensive, polished, perfectly grained oak casket
lowered inside the bronzed, watertight vault
lowered into the minutely turning earth.

A few shovelsful of dirt.
A child's rose.

Sun emerging from behind clouds.

Later, rain.

*

Certainty's a luxury.

Never having had it, I've nothing to teach you.

There's nothing about me
                     of Orpheus, or Augustine, or Jonathan Edwards

on the steps of whose old church
I used to wait for the bus home to Nowheresville.

Even my name's not mine.

It's been a tough hitchhike to here.

A couple more light-years maybe I'll be ready.

OF CATS, SWITCHBLADES
& THE UNIMAGINABLE

                        Brass-light.
            Autumnal late July.

The sun's already shifting south.

            My Buddha looks thin this morning.

                    *

To be prince of nobodies, one of the know-nothings.

To achieve that.

                    *

1949.

Five bony kids, ex-GI's,
with crooked teeth and hooked noses,

lounging outside Beckman's in Northampton, Mass.

Wearing pegs and spread-collar shirts in peach or lavender,
the tie in a double Windsor,

the cardigan jacket.

Cats with bright links,
shooting our cuffs and waiting for the girls to happen.

Jiving on Saturday nights at Mountain Park Ballroom.

Switch-blades, Diz.

Oh, cool.

*

Drifting toward the unimagined future.

The Unimaginable.

*

Chesterfields. Luckies.

At the out of tune piano
            in the lobby of the old Holyoke red-brick mansion YMCA,

the cigarette between the lips or between the fingers,
slender ribbon of smoke, pale blue satin, riffling up.

*

Drifting toward a music, a style. Toward grace. Toward a *raison d'etre.*

*

So many versions of the self still to go.

Variation after variation.

Each the fiction of a fiction.

Down to the final fiction.

*

Oh, sparrow! I've seen you, breast ripped open,
the sad little rigging of your bones, the bloody flesh.

Fluster and bluster of The Great Oz
                    when the curtain's finally drawn back.

*

Cat under a tree in the heat.

                              Smoke in shadow.

The shape of the end of the shovel handle,
           the shape of the soreness in the palm of my hand.

Red badge. Cracked nails.

Cat have talent. He sing. He don't do shit-work.

How come he smarter than is us alls?

LATE OCTOBER RAINY DAYS

Almost November.
Light the color and heft of lead.

Air raw with rain.

Last night, in a single swoon,
my neighbor's ash dropped

all its leaves at once
in a weave thick and intricate —

one only some dreaming Emir's
Persian carpet-master might dare —

green, brown, yellow-gold, plum.

*

Days like this,
I sometimes turn off all my study lights
and box the darkness in.

One lamp burning over my old black Selectric
like firelight.

Its heart humming.

*

Yesterday,

                     for miles in every direction,

clouds of starlings ballooned, veering & twittering,
over cornfield & beanfield,

weedrow & swale.

Exfoliating. Infolding. Ribboning.

Black as a dictionary.
Black as the wobble at the pivot of your gaze.

There and not there.

Itself and the other.
Making and unmaking.
                              Metadimensional.

A language all its own.

Congregation & ikon.

                    *

Early evening,

the sun has finally returned

surprising sky, houses, trees, the neighborhood's scraggy lawns,
with fresh color.

Spanging gold off west-facing windows.

Its reflected light
mellowing down to the hue of the last of your last good scotch.

Birds homing to every bush and tree.

Little ones.
Bright eyes.

We earn our keep.

IN HEAVEN

Living at the edges, I grow stranger.

Heaven is here, I think, not there. There is no there there,
as Gertrude Stein said of her old hometown.

> No congress of souls.
> No fire and ice.

> *

Two days after the autumn equinox,
> last full week in September,

two cloudless nights under harvest moons,
> the cinnamon fern turning brown,

the wind in the high canopy of our hundred year old oaks,
their still green leaves tossing and veering,
> a foil of shining lit by the six o'clock sun.

> *

Except for the persistent smack and wash and grind
of the Interstate,

we'd have no sense of the Empire,
> its markets falling and wasted.

> *

My neighbors' long-legged half-golden-retriever yaps happily
amid the red and golden delicious left to rot on sidewalk and lawn.

> Bruised here. Worm-holed there.

Pecker-fretted and cidery. Nectar for marauding bees.

*

My president's a demagogue and a fool.
A man who's failed upward from privilege to privilege.
An expensive suit on a broken stick in an autumn field.

*

And so, this evening, my country stutters toward a war it doesn't want.

It wants this sweet wind.
It wants its sons and daughters alive and whole.
It wants a diplomacy elegant as wings.

Let the mullahs and CEO's
cry out in dust and blood.

This will still be the garden.
Its household gods the ant, the wood mouse, and the wren.
The trees its angels, engines of breath.

This last light slanting through shadow,
firing the red and orange of twiggy bittersweet in a milk glass vase,

the basket of red tomatoes,
the sullen unripe pears, green and blushing in their bowl,

will still stream and sing,

waste it how we will.

TEN THOUSAND WINGBEATS
FIVE HUNDRED HEARTBEATS

Cloud-buffalo grazing a thousand miles of blue range.

Day dry as a biscuit.

Snap your fingers and start a forest fire.

*

Water ouzel
Underwater walker   waddler   clear-singing dipper bird & dripper

I saw once.

A long time ago.

*

We're far from the Eastern Court, Wu Wei said,
where poetry's princelings hum & muddle.

Some.

No Yippee-yi-yay, Yippee-yi-yo. Kuma-ti-yi-yippee-yippee-yay.

No breaks. No sashay.

Just do-si-do.

*

Start from where you are.

Below the kitchen window,
ledgers of rock.

Journals tossed on a slow-sliding pile.

Fire-blackened & yellowed. On one, the rust-red seal of algae.

Rain-soaked books of a ruined library.

*

My own lines ground down to gravel.

*

Stumbles of sand & pink quartz.
Scruff of bitterbush.

Two lean coyote hurrying along a deerpath a little above.

*

Whistle & slap & whirr of hummingbirds.

Green black ruby iridescences of raku or cloisonné.

Wings beating 10,000 strokes a minute 500 heartbeats
                                    at our red-tin-can feeder.

*

Angry jewels of the air.

Whose treasure are they?

STEPPING LIGHTLY

This day is the edge we live on.

From which we wager out & back, out & back.

Walking on air. Walking on water.

Our luck holding. Mostly.

*

And there are touches like several sorts of silk, like satin.
Warm breath kissing our bodies.
Touches like a run of icicles.

Touches like stone, coarse and bruising.

Just ask me,
Old Fumblefingers, tugging at your buttons.

*

This morning, spring snow bundles the woods.

And soon all the beautiful sleepers will awake

and the sun break it all down to brilliance.

*

Some days fatigue licks my shoes.

*

"There is no fascism like the fascism of the young," my friend said.

That was long ago
        walking down Grand Avenue on a sunlit day in Detroit.

Apropos of something long forgotten now.

                            *

And who are you?
            Who are you? And you?
        I want to ask the faces behind the windows of passing cars,

the walkers on streets and in parking lots,

            the girl at the Target checkout.

How many months, years

would it take to know you, how many stories
told over and over and then retold?

To be listened to over and over.

All those years I once had I no longer have
                            in which to listen.

Another lost life-work.
                    *

Woe unto small lives.

        Little Miss Greenheart is dying.

Woe unto the joy and magic of our small cat.
        Black-grey and white mischief.

She who spanks the surface of the water in the bowl.

The small animal with green eyes who drinks from her right paw

and speaks a language of one coarse syllable.

She who, at night, sleeps bouldered against your ankle
or warm behind the deep bend of your knees.

Woe of sudden cancer.

Dumb death in a language she does not understand.

And so she goes about her day,
the pennant of her tail-tip flying — east wind, west wind.

Small sweet courage,
going about its muscular business.

*

Oh, my love.

What shall we do with our grief and anger?

What shall I do with the howl twisting through my witless head.

The black sun sinks slowly down the white sky of her back
into the dark waters,

an oil slick moon sliding black and bright

across her right shoulder.

*

You show me
         your God of love and mercy.

And I'll show you
         the God of wasting away.

*

At the end of darkness is darkness.

*

I'm off now,
        down
some moonless fractal, wild refraction, unpredictable reflection.

Starless.

Stepping lightly.

CHIMES

Mid-August. Evening. Rain falling.

Cold, bright silk where the street fronts the house.

Out back, it laves and slicks the parched leaves of the trees.
Ragged hang of summer's end.

I lean against the doorway of the poem,
listening to the old patter.

My cat, Zeke, lays himself out imperially.
Eleven pounds of grey smoke
                    with tufted ears and a curved plume of tail.

Now, a slight wind,
and The Emperor of Heaven's chimes intone like distant bells,
his court musician's 4000-year-old pentatonic scale
                    pealing in slow, clear ripples.

Occasionally, a chord.

Every day I live I live forever.

NOTES

THE FIGURES
Book of Hours. A collection of spiritual meditations, usually by monks, although the best known may be Rilke's.

GARDEN FABLE
Aristoxenus. Mentioned in *The Complete Greek Cookbook*, Theresa Karas Yialnilos, 1970.

ECSTASY
White Lady. A variety of peach characterized by pale flesh and a profusion of light, sweet juice.

EXIT
The Grand Army Highway. Named for The Grand Army of the Republic, a society founded in 1866 of Civil War veterans who had served in the Union army.

UNDER THE FROST MOON
Frost Moon. A colloquial term for the full moon that occurs in November

THE KNOT
Celtic Knot. A complex, multi-corded knot, often four- or six-cornered, of mystical significance.

IN PANAMA
Linnaeus. Carolus Linnaeus. Original name, Carl von Linne. Swedish botanist and originator of the system of taxonomic classification (by genus, species, etc.).

KALIBAN ON ESTERO
Honeybell. A large grapefruit-tangerine hybrid, thin-skinned, mostly seedless, and full of very sweet juice.

SPINDRIFT
Heebie-Jeebies. A feeling of uneasiness, nervousness. Coined by Billy De Beck (1890-1942), American cartoonist, in his comic strip *Barney Google.*

Cage. John Cage. American composer of experimental music, 1912-1992.

TROPIC FREEZE
Dhawo. First mentioned by D. Morrill in a monograph on Alfred Hitchcock in *Cinematographia del Sud*, 1926.

Panatela. A long, slender cigar.

Dinch. A regional English dialect word for shovel.

CHIMES
Emperor of Heaven. Shih Huang Ti. Legendary first Emperor of China. Believed to have ordered the construction of The Great Wall.

TEN THOUSAND WINGBEATS FIVE HUNDRED HEARTBEATS
Wu wei. "Not Doing." A principle of Zen, as taught by the Chinese master Hsu Yun. See *The Practice of Zen*, Chang Chen, 1960. In the poem, the word is deliberately conflated with the name of a poet of the late T'ang period.

Raku. A method in which bisqued and glazed pottery is removed directly to a pit and covered with straw, leaves, and/or wood chips. The method intensifies colors and often gives the pots a rainbow iridescence.

Cloisonné. A method of decorating the surfaces of jewelry, vases, and boxes, using enamels separated by metal strips and heated together at high temperatures. A technique invented by oriental artisans and later borrowed by the French.

ABOUT THE AUTHOR

Robert Dana was born in Boston in 1929. After serving in the South Pacific at the end of World War II, he moved to Iowa where he attended Drake University and The University of Iowa Writers' Workshop. His poetry has won several awards including two National Endowment for the Arts Fellowships and The Delmore Schwartz Memorial Award from New York University. Retired from teaching after forty years as Poet-in-Residence at Cornell College, he has also served as Distinguished Visiting Writer at Stockholm University and at several American colleges and universities. His earlier books include *What I Think I Know: New and Selected Poems*; *Yes, Everything*; *Hello, Stranger;* and *Summer.*